Copyright © 2023

All Rights Reserved.

No part of this publication may be reproduced, distributed, or transmitted in any form or by any means. Including photocopying, recording, or other electronic ormechanical methods, without the prior written permission of the publisher, expect in the case of the brief quotations embodied in critical reviews and certain other non-commercial uses permitted by copyright law.

Don't forget to
Give Thank's

This Book Belongs To:

_____

_____

I Spy with my little eye
Something beginning with ...

I spy with my little eye
Something beginning with ...

A

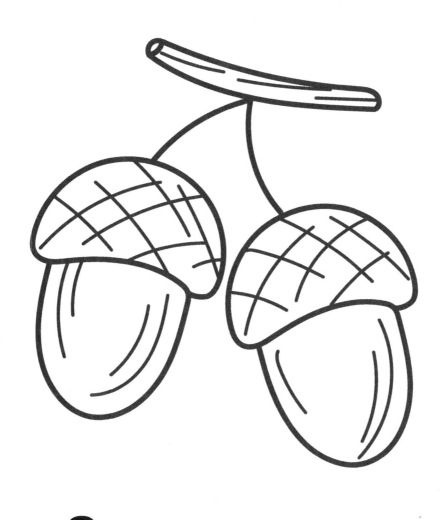

Acorns

I Spy with my little eye
Something beginning with ...

B

Buns

I Spy with my little eye
Something beginning with ...

I spy with my little eye
Something beginning with...

C

Corn

I Spy with my little eye
Something beginning with ...

D

I spy with my little eye
Something beginning with...

Duck

I Spy with my little eye
Something beginning with ...

Elf

I Spy with my little eye Something beginning with ...

I spy with my little eye
Something beginning with...

F

Fox

Fox

I Spy with my little eye
Something beginning with ...

Gravy

I Spy with my little eye
Something beginning with ...

I spy with my little eye
Something beginning with ...

H

Ham

I Spy with my little eye
Something beginning with ...

Ice cream

ice cream

I Spy with my little eye
Something beginning with ...

I Spy with my little eye
Something beginning with ...

Jacket

I Spy with my little eye
Something beginning with ...

K

I spy with my little eye
Something beginning with ...

Kettle

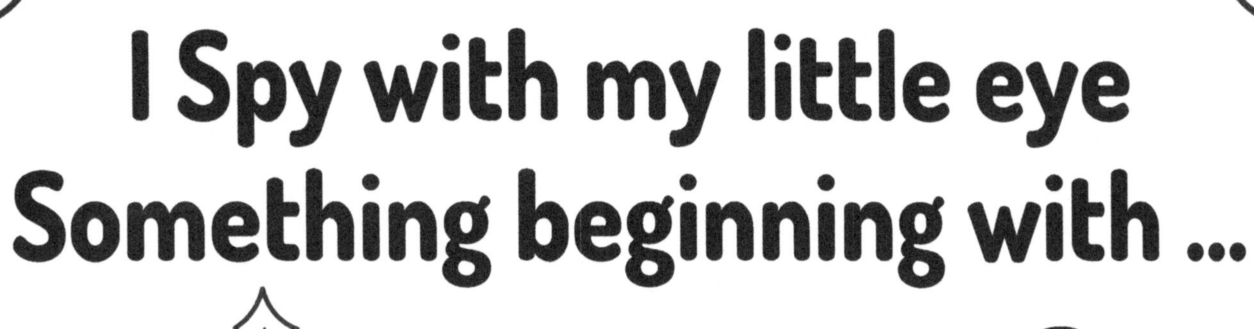

I Spy with my little eye
Something beginning with ...

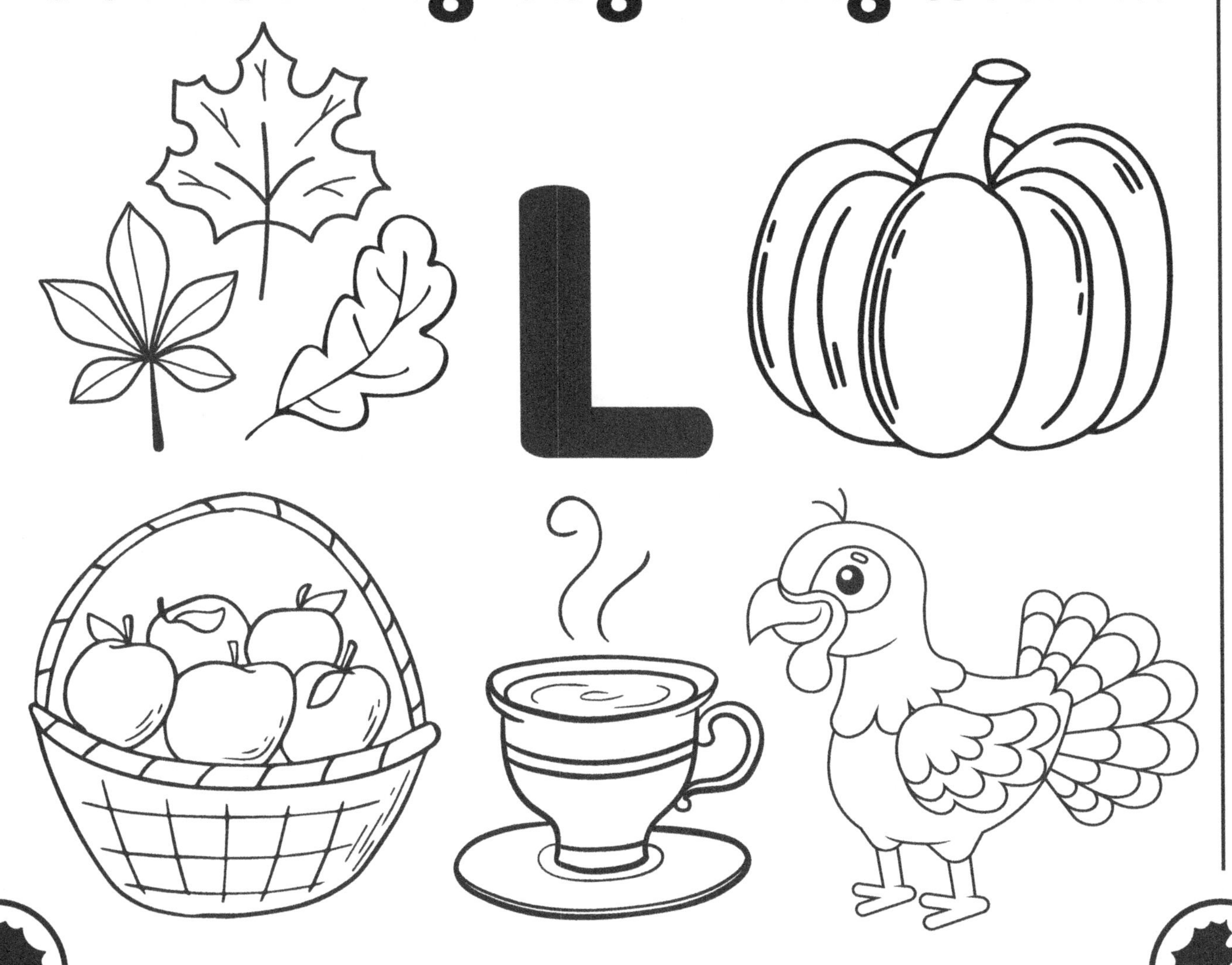

I Spy with my little eye
Something beginning with...

Leaves

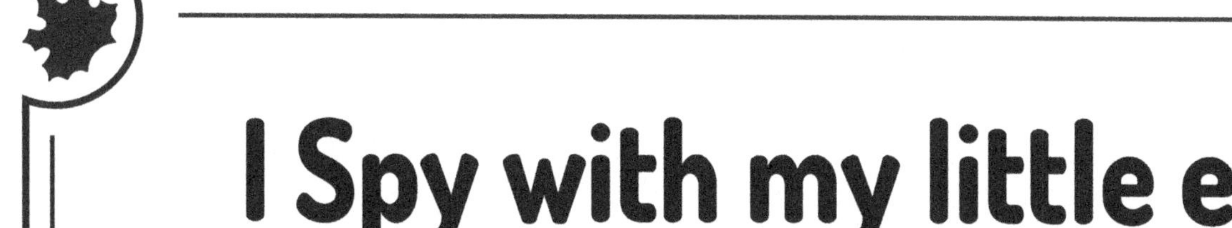

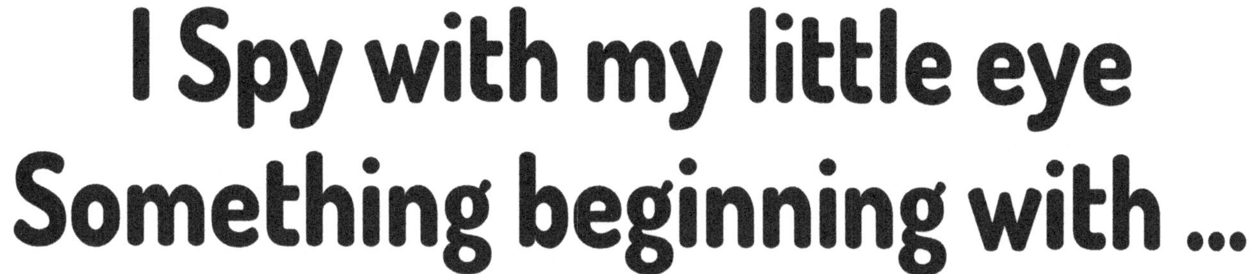

I Spy with my little eye
Something beginning with ...

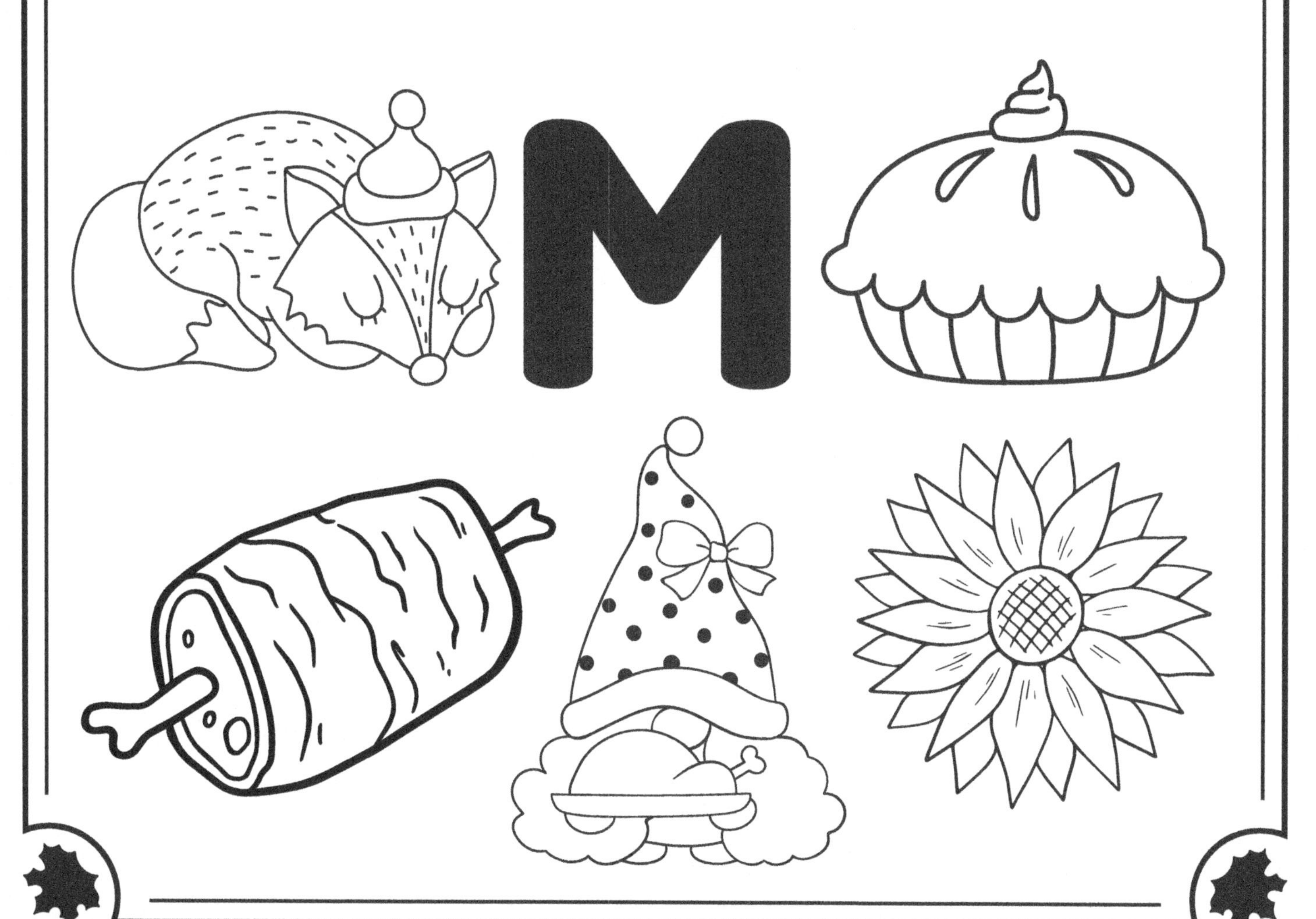

I Spy with my little eye
Something beginning with ...

M

Meat

I Spy with my little eye Something beginning with ...

I spy with my little eye

Something beginning with ...

N

Nest

I Spy with my little eye
Something beginning with ...

O

I Spy with my little eye
Something beginning with ...

Owl

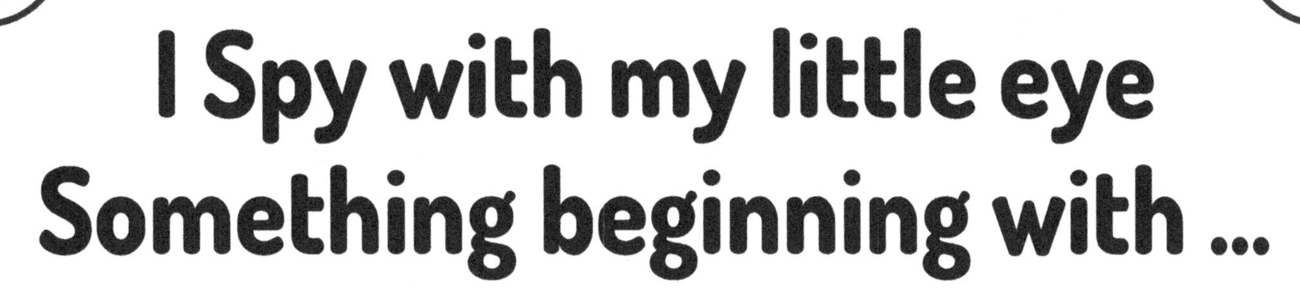

I Spy with my little eye
Something beginning with ...

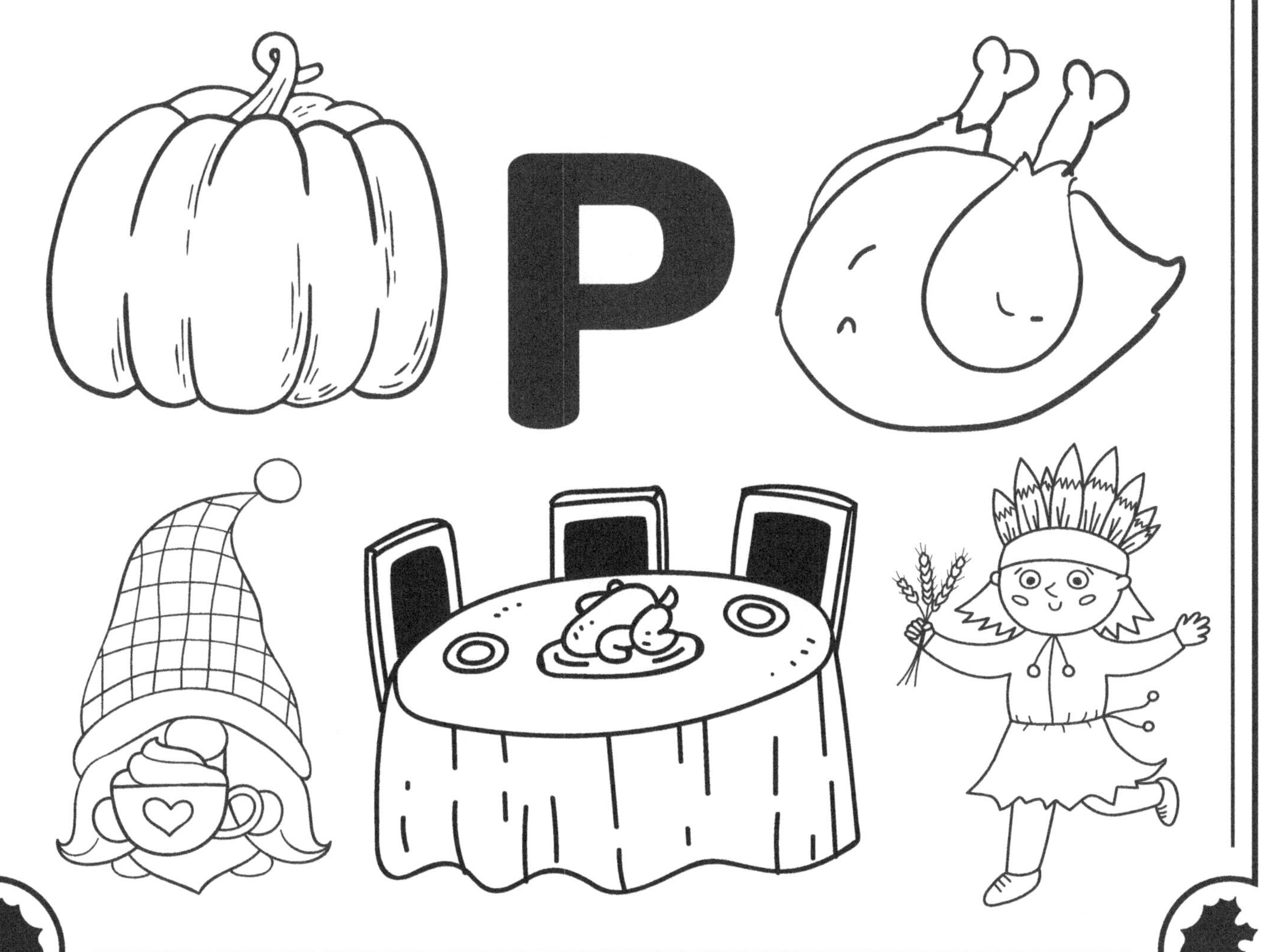

I Spy with my little eye
Something beginning with ...

Pumpkin

I Spy with my little eye
Something beginning with ...

I spy with my little eye
Something beginning with ...

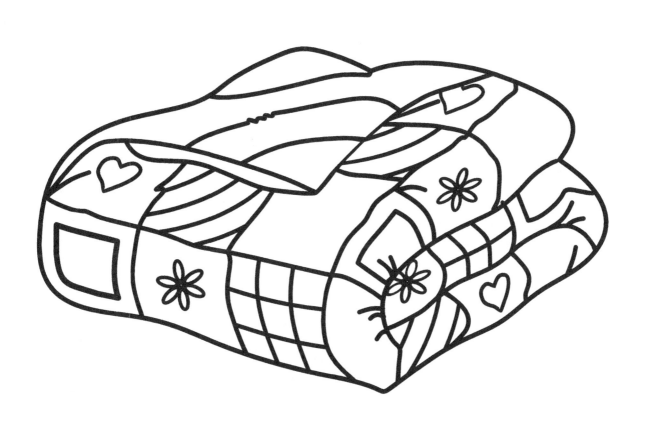

Quilt

I Spy with my little eye
Something beginning with ...

I Spy with my little eye
Something beginning with ...

R

Roast

I Spy with my little eye
Something beginning with ...

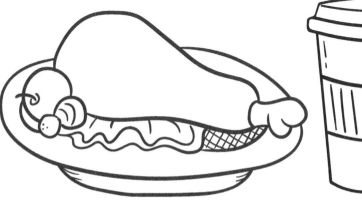

I spy with my little eye
Something beginning with ...

Squirrel

I Spy with my little eye Something beginning with ...

Turkey

I Spy with my little eye
Something beginning with ...

Unicorn

I Spy with my little eye Something beginning with ...

V

I spy with my little eye
Something beginning with ...

V

Vegetables

I Spy with my little eye
Something beginning with ...

I spy with my little eye
Something beginning with...

W

Wagon

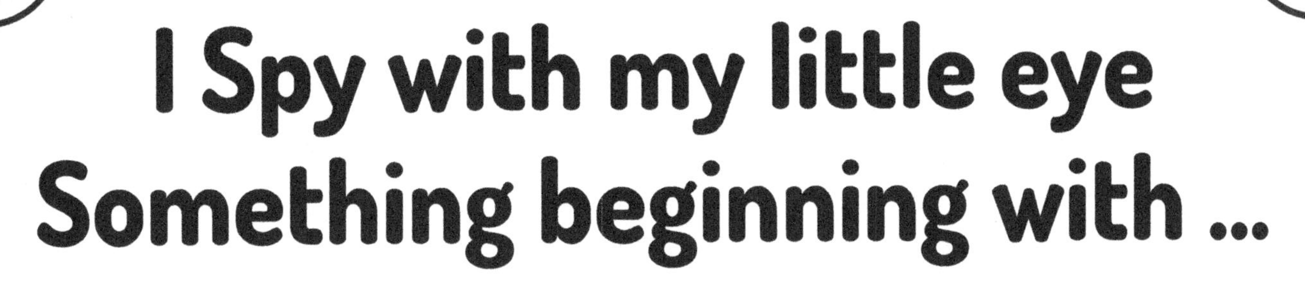

I Spy with my little eye
Something beginning with ...

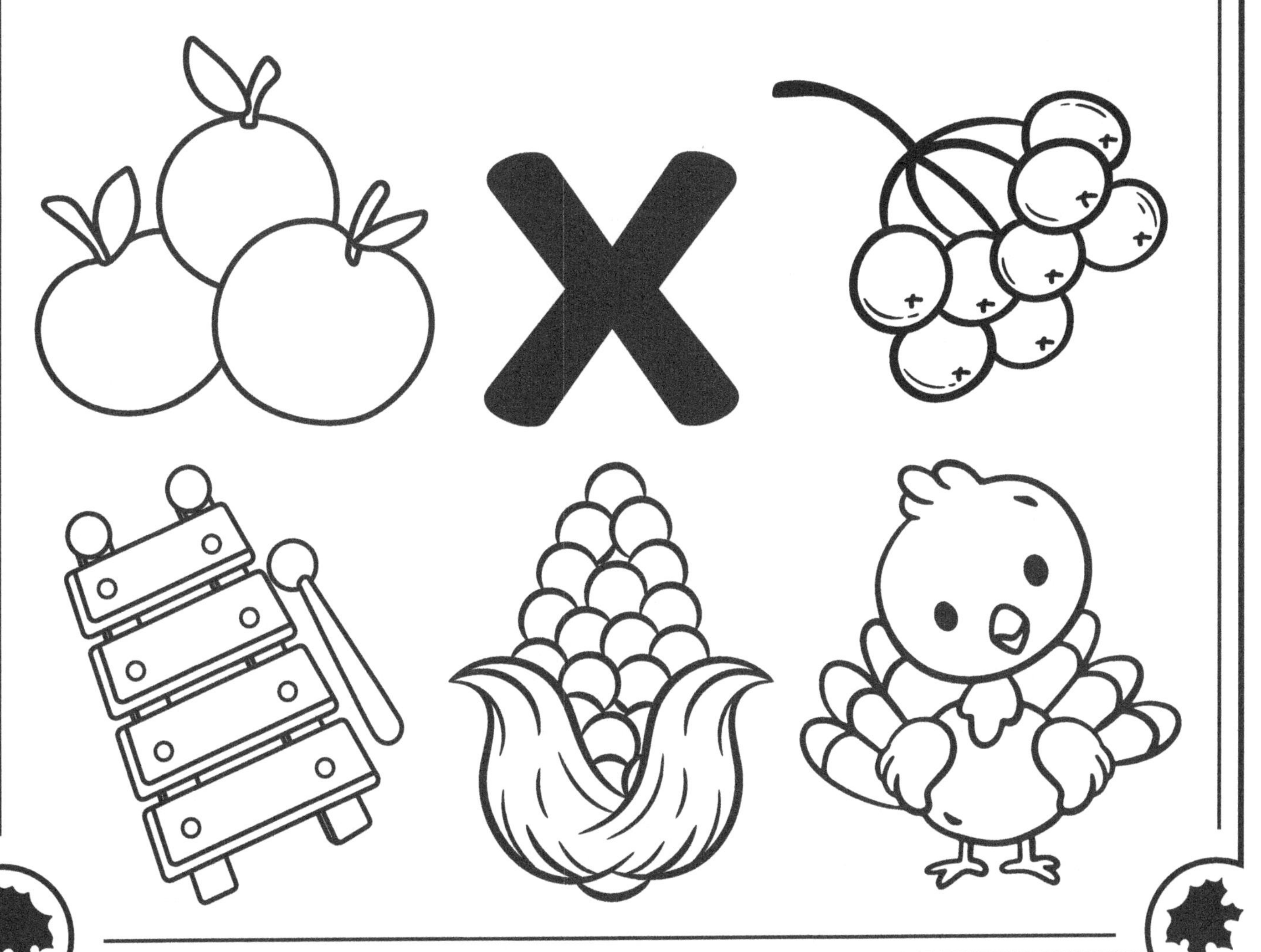

I spy with my little eye
Something beginning with ...

Xylophone

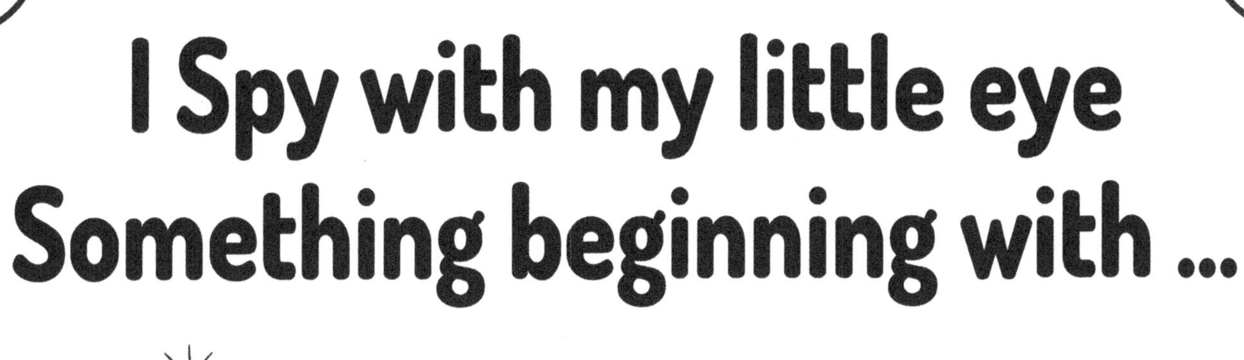

I Spy with my little eye
Something beginning with ...

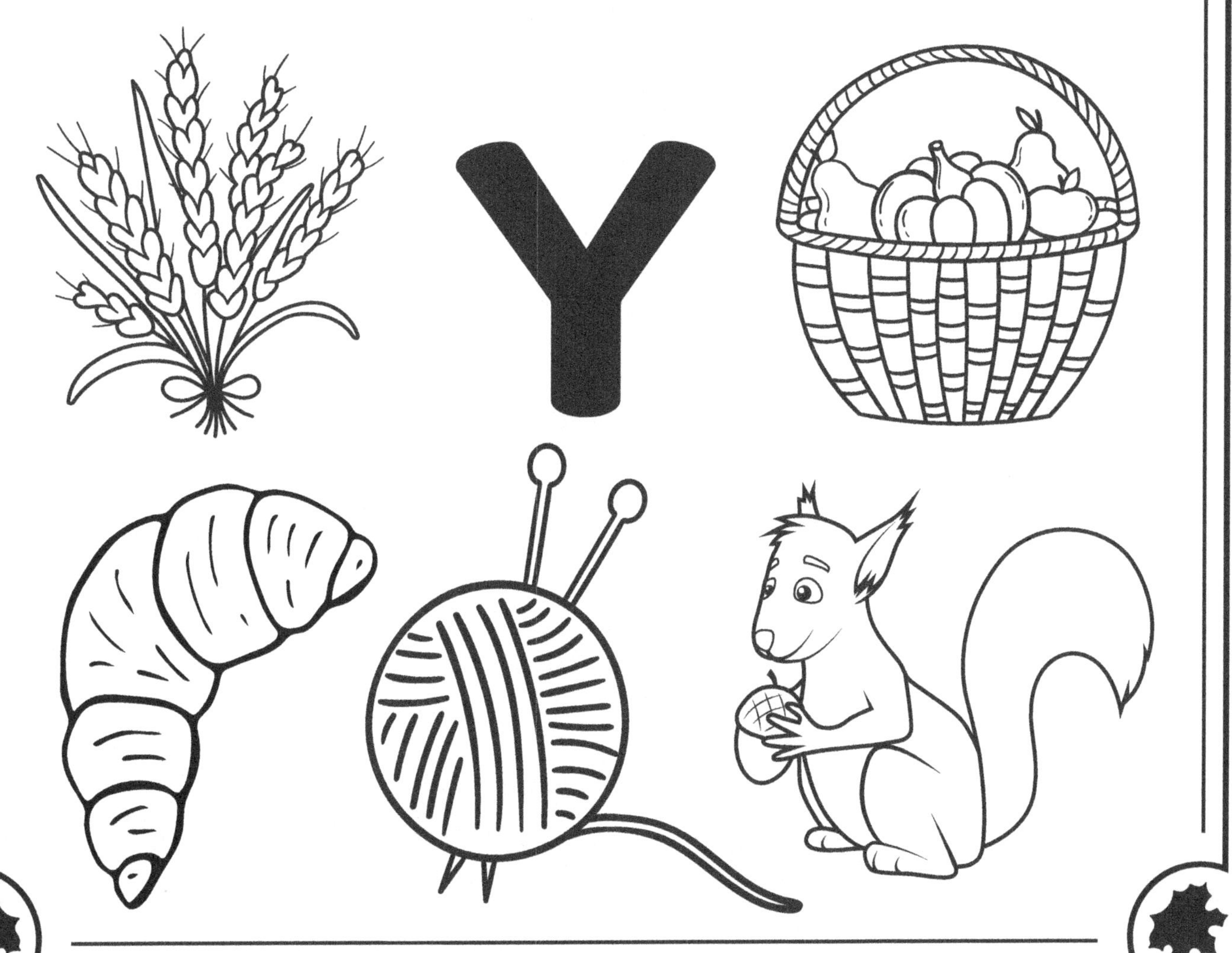

I Spy with my little eye
Something beginning with ...

Y

Yarn

I Spy with my little eye
Something beginning with ...

I Spy with my little eye
Something beginning with...

Zebra

HAPPY Thanksgiving

I hope you enjoyed ♡

Support our work by leaving us

Good Feedback!

Discover more fun books in

Our store "Flora Wenna"

Made in the USA
Monee, IL
30 October 2024

68974507R00059